13-Digit ISBN: 978-1-60433-275-9
10-Digit ISBN: 1-60433-275-1

This book may be ordered by mail from the publisher. Please include $2.95 for postage and handling. Please support your local bookseller first!

Books published by Cider Mill Press Book Publishers are available at special discounts for bulk purchases in the United States by corporations, institutions, and other organizations. For more information, please contact the publisher.

Applesauce Press is an imprint of
Cider Mill Press Book Publishers
"Where good books are ready for press"
12 Port Farm Road
Kennebunkport, Maine 04046

Visit us on the Web!
www.cidermillpress.com

Design by Tilly Grassa - TGCreative Services
All illustrations courtesy of Anthony Owsley

1 2 3 4 5 6 7 8 9 0
First Edition

CONTENTS

CHAPTER
1
Things That Go Knock! Knock! in the Night

Knock! Knock!
Who's there?
Logan.
Logan who?
Logan see if there's a full moon out.

* *

KNOCK! KNOCK!
WHO'S THERE?
ZELDA.
ZELDA WHO?
ZELDA HOUSE!
I THINK IT'S HAUNTED.

* * * * * * * * * * *

Knock! Knock!
Who's there?
I scream.
I scream who?
I scream tastes cool on
a hot day.

* *

Knock! Knock!
Who's there?
Weaver.
Weaver who?
Weaver alone, you horrible monster!

Knock! Knock!
Who's there?
Shepherd.
Shepherd who?
Shepherd a monster outside, didn't you sheep?

****

KNOCK! KNOCK!
WHO'S THERE?
EERIE.
EERIE WHO?
EERIE GO AGAIN!

Knock! Knock!
Who's there?
Karlof.
Karlof who?
Karlof your dogs, monster hunters.
I surrender.

Knock! Knock!
Who's there?
Egypt.
Egypt who?
Egypt me when he sold me this phony magic potion.

KNOCK! KNOCK!
WHO'S THERE?
OOZE.
OOZE WHO?
OOZE AFRAID OF
MONSTERS? NOT ME!

Knock! Knock!
Who's there?
Wheelbarrow.
Wheelbarrow who?
Wheelbarrow your
bloodhounds to track down Dracula.

Knock! Knock!
Who's there?
Weird.
Weird who?
Weird you hide the monster you
made last night?

Knock! Knock!
Who's there?
Wail.
Wail who?
Wail find your monster if we have to search
every inch of your castle.

Knock! Knock!
Who's there?
Talon.
Talon who?
Talon monster stories scares little kids.

• •

Knock! Knock!
Who's there?
I'm Gladys.
I'm Gladys who?
I'm Gladys spooky story is finally over.

• •

Knock! Knock!
Who's there?
Ditty.
Ditty who?
Ditty see a monster outside or not?

• •

Knock! Knock!
Who's there?
Sheena.
Sheena who?
Have you Sheena big ugly monster around here?

KNOCK! KNOCK!
WHO'S THERE?
DOUGHNUT.
DOUGHNUT WHO?
DOUGHNUT GO TO
DRACULA'S CASTLE
AFTER SUNSET.

Knock! Knock!
Who's there?
Wilma.
Wilma who?
Wilma howling keep you awake all night?

KNOCK! KNOCK!
WHO'S THERE?
ZEALOUS.
ZEALOUS WHO?
ZEALOUS AN AMULET TO PROTECT US
FROM VAMPIRES.

Knock! Knock!
Who's there?
Dewey.
Dewey who?
Dewey have enough garlic to
repel a vampire attack?

Knock! Knock!
Who's there?
Welcome.
Welcome who?
Welcome to your rescue if vampires attack.

KNOCK! KNOCK!
WHO'S THERE?
ACHOO.
ACHOO WHO?
ACHOO ON PEOPLE'S NECKS, SAID THE VAMPIRE.

Knock! Knock!
Who's there?
Shirley.
Shirley who?
Shirley you're not afraid of vampires.

Knock! Knock!
Who's there?
It's a waffle.
It's a waffle who?
It's a waffle sight to see—
zombies walking around.

SYYYRRRRUP!

Knock! Knock!
Who's there?
Menu.
Menu who?
Menu see Count Dracula, protect your neck.

KNOCK! KNOCK!

WHO'S THERE?

HAROLD.

HAROLD WHO?

HAROLD IS COUNT DRACULA? I BET HE'S AT LEAST ONE HUNDRED YEARS OLD.

Knock! Knock!
Who's there?
Cheese.
Cheese who?
Cheese kind of cute even if she is a vampire.

Knock! Knock!
Who's there?
Cement.
Cement who?
Cement to scream when she saw Dracula, but she fainted instead.

Knock! Knock!
Who's there?
Vein.
Vein who?
Vein you go to Dracula's castle be sure to wear garlic around your neck.

Knock! Knock!
Who's there?
Lena.
Lena who?
Lena little closer. I want to bite your neck.

KNOCK! KNOCK!
WHO'S THERE?
ZOMBIES.
ZOMBIES WHO?
ZOMBIES GATHER HONEY WHILE OTHERS GUARD THE HIVE.

Knock! Knock!
Who's there?
Candice.
Candice who?
Candice zombie be brought back to life?

Knock! Knock!
Who's there?
I'm Cher.
I'm Cher who?
I'm Cher afraid of zombies.

KNOCK! KNOCK!
WHO'S THERE?
WENDY.
WENDY WHO?
WENDY FULL MOON RISES, WEREWOLVES START
TO PROWL AROUND.

Knock! Knock!
Who's there?
Obscene.
Obscene who?
Obscene men change into wolves
when the full moon rises.

Knock! Knock!
Who's there?
Voodoo.
Voodoo who?
Voodoo you think is more
dangerous, Dracula or Wolfman?

Knock! Knock!
Who's there?
Decry.
Decry who?
Decry of the Wolfman sends
shivers down my spine.
****

Knock! Knock!
Who's there?
Defer.
Defer who?
Defer coat of a werewolf
is very thick.

****

KNOCK! KNOCK!
WHO'S THERE?
EYELID.
EYELID WHO?
EYELID A SECRET LIFE AS A WEREWOLF.
****
Knock! Knock!
Who's there?
Dozen.
Dozen who?
Dozen anyone believe I was
chased by a werewolf?

Knock! Knock!
Who's there?
Hubie.
Hubie who?
Hubie in before the full moon rises
or a werewolf might get you.

● ●

KNOCK! KNOCK!

WHO'S THERE?

DRAGON.

DRAGON WHO?

DRAGON YOUR FEET WILL GET YOUR

SHOES DIRTY.

Knock! Knock!
Who's there?
Clara.
Clara who?
Clara path! Here's comes a monster and I'm
out of here!

Knock! Knock!
Who's there?
Teller.
Teller who?
Teller to scream loud if she sees a monster.

Knock! Knock!
Who's there?
Hour.
Hour who?
Hour we going to destroy that monster?

Knock! Knock!
Who's there?
Barn.
Barn who?
Barn down Frankenstein's castle.

Knock! Knock!
Who's there?
Gargoyle.
Gargoyle who?
Gargoyle with mouthwash. You have bat breath.

Knock! Knock!
Who's there?
Witch Doctor.
Witch Doctor who?
Witch Doctor do you recommend for this operation?

Knock! Knock!
Who's there?
Alp!
Alp who?
Alp me. A yeti is after me.

KNOCK! KNOCK!
WHO'S THERE?
ICY.
ICY WHO?
ICY A MONSTER HIDING IN THE BUSHES.

Knock! Knock!
Who's there?
Value.
Value who?
Value stop growling at me already.

Knock! Knock!
Who's there?
Uriah.
Uriah who?
Uriah is kind of red, Mr. Cyclops.

Knock! Knock!
Who's there?
Candy.
Candy who?
Candy monster you
created breathe fire?

. . . .

Knock! Knock!
Who's there?
Thumb.
Thumb who?
Thumb folks like horror movies. I don't.

Knock! Knock!
Who's there?
I spider.
I spider who?
I spider sneaking around our secret
laboratory.

Knock! Knock!
Who's there?
Willis.
Willis who?
Willis nightmare ever end?

CHAPTER **2**
Animal Crack-Ups

Knock! Knock!
Who's there?
I adder.
I adder who?
I adder in a trap, but she escaped.

****

Knock! Knock!
Who's there?
Gecko.
Gecko who?
Gecko-ing or you'll be late for school.

KNOCK! KNOCK!
WHO'S THERE?
WEASEL.
WEASEL WHO?
WEASEL WHILE YOU WORK.

Knock! Knock!
Who's there?
Lassie.
Lassie who?
Lassie what's on the cable channels.

Knock! Knock!
Who's there?
Gopher.
Gopher who?
Gopher a walk to calm your nerves.

****

Knock! Knock!
Who's there?
Rabbit.
Rabbit who?
Rabbit up. It's an order to go.

• •

KNOCK! KNOCK!
WHO'S THERE?
ODOR.
ODOR WHO?
ODOR SKUNKS ARE WISER THAN
YOUNGER SKUNKS.

Knock! Knock!
Who's there?
Distinct.
Distinct who?
Distinct of a skunk is awful.

KNOCK! KNOCK!
WHO'S THERE?
POSSUM.
POSSUM WHO?
POSSUM SOME RELISH ON HIS HOTDOG.

Knock! Knock!
Who's there?
Hyena.
Hyena who?
Hyena tree sits the majestic eagle.

Knock! Knock!
Who's there?
Lion.
Lion who?
Lion will get you into trouble, so be truthful.

Knock! Knock!
Who's there?
Lion.
Lion who?
Lion on a block of ice can send shivers down your spine.

Knock! Knock!
Who's there?
Thea.
Thea who?
Thea later alligator!

Knock! Knock!
Who's there?
Poodle.
Poodle who?
Poodle little mustard
on my hot dog.

KNOCK! KNOCK!
WHO'S THERE?
WOODCHUCK.
WOODCHUCK WHO?
WOODCHUCK COME TO OUR PARTY IF WE
INVITED HIM?

Knock! Knock!
Who's there?
Gibbon.
Gibbon who?
Gibbon is always better than
receiving.

Knock! Knock!
Who's there?
A rattle.
A rattle who?
A rattle squeal on his friends every time.

KNOCK! KNOCK!
WHO'S THERE?
ASP.
ASP WHO?
ASP YOUR MOTHER IF YOU CAN COME OUT.

Knock! Knock!
Who's there?
Whale.
Whale who?
Whale I guess I'll be going now.

Knock! Knock!
Who's there?
Gopher.
Gopher who?
Gopher a snack while the commercial's on.

Knock! Knock!
Who's there?
Harry.
Harry who?
Harry up. I don't want to miss the elephant parade.

● ● ● ● ● ● ● ● ● ● ● ● ● ● ● ● ● ● ●

Knock! Knock!
Who's there?
Who?
Who Who?
What are you,
some kind of
owl?

Who?

● ● ● ● ● ● ● ● ● ● ●

Knock! Knock!
Who's there?
Howell.
Howell who?
Howell I feed my pet elephant?

● ●

KNOCK! KNOCK!
WHO'S THERE?
DOZEN.
DOZEN WHO?
DOZEN ANYONE WANT TO SEE THE
CIRCUS ELEPHANTS?

Knock! Knock!
Who's there?
Ella.
Ella who?
Ellaphant.

KNOCK! KNOCK!
WHO'S THERE?
OWL.
OWL WHO?
OWL BE BACK IN A MINUTE.

****

Knock! Knock!
Who's there?
Ammonia.
Ammonia who?
Ammonia bird in a cage.

****

Knock! Knock!
Who's there?
Wottle.
Wottle who?
Wottle I do now? asked the turkey.

Knock! Knock!
Who's there?
Egos.
Egos who?
Egos are big birds with keen eyesight.

• • • • • • • • • • • • • • •

Knock! Knock!
Who's there?
Hens.
Hens who?
Hens up!
We've got you
surrounded.

* * * * * * * * * * * *

Knock! Knock!
Who's there?
A bird talon.
A bird talon who?
A bird talon fibs is a serious matter.

* *

Knock! Knock!
Who's there?
Wren.
Wren who?
Wren in Rome, do as the
Romans do.

Knock! Knock!
Who's there?
Wren.
Wren who?
Wren you're smiling, the whole world smiles with you.

KNOCK! KNOCK!
WHO'S THERE?
N-M-T
N-M-T WHO?
N-M-T NEST MAKES A MOTHER BIRD SAD.

Knock! Knock!
Who's there?
Cayuse.
Cayuse who?
Cayuse your bathroom? I gotta go.

Knock! Knock!
Who's there?
Mare E.
Mare E. who?
Mare E. Christmas everyone!

KNOCK! KNOCK!
WHO'S THERE?
KEN L.
KEN L. WHO?
KEN L.S ARE DOG HOTELS.

Knock! Knock!
Who's there?
Tabby.
Tabby who?
Tabby or not tabby, that is the question.

Knock! Knock!
Who's there?
Irish.
Irish who?
Irish your dog would stop barking.

KNOCK! KNOCK!
WHO'S THERE?
COINCIDE.
COINCIDE WHO?
COINCIDE AND LET THE DOG OUT.

KNOCK! KNOCK!
WHO'S THERE?
SHEENA.
SHEENA WHO?
SHEENA LOST DOG AROUND HERE?

* * * * * * * * * * * * * * * * * *

Knock! Knock!
Who's there?
Noah kitten.
Noah kitten who?
Noah kitten who wants to play with me?

KNOCK! KNOCK!
WHO'S THERE?
DESIGN.
DESIGN WHO?
DESIGN SAID BEWARE OF DOG!

* * * * * * * * * * * * * * * * * * * *

Knock! Knock!
Who's there?
Kit.
Kit who?
Kit busy and stop asking
silly questions.

Knock! Knock!
Who's there?
Ty.
Ty who?
**Ty up the dog before he
runs away.**

* * * * * * * * * * * * * * * * * * * *

KNOCK! KNOCK!
WHO'S THERE?
ANNETTE.
ANNETTE WHO?
ANNETTE IS USED TO CATCH STRAY DOGS.

* * * * * * * * * * * * * * * * * * * *

Knock! Knock!
Who's there?
I Major.
I Major who?
I Major watchdog run away.

* * * * * * * * * *

KNOCK! KNOCK!
WHO'S THERE?
OX.
OX WHO?
OX ME NICE AND I'LL
TAKE YOU OUT FOR
ICE CREAM.

Knock! Knock!
Who's there?
Eject.
Eject who?
Eject the chicken coop and all the hens are gone.

****

KNOCK! KNOCK!
WHO'S THERE?
MULE.
MULE WHO?
MULE BE SORRY IF YOU DON'T OPEN THE DOOR.

Knock! Knock!
Who's there?
Pig.
Pig who?
Pig me up at five o'clock.

****

Knock! Knock!
Who's there?
Hence.
Hence who?
Hence lay eggs in chicken coops.

KNOCK! KNOCK!
WHO'S THERE?
COW.
COW WHO?
COW MUCH LONGER ARE YOU GOING TO PUT
UP WITH ALL THIS KNOCKING?

• •

Knock! Knock!
Who's there?
A cow pasture.
A cow pasture who?
A cow pasture house on its way to the barn.

* *

Knock! Knock!
Who's there?
Sty.
Sty who?
Sty home from school if you feel ill.

Knock! Knock!
Who's there?
Pig.
Pig who?
Pig on someone your own size.

Knock! Knock!
Who's there?
Aware, aware.
Aware, aware who?
Aware, aware has my little dog gone?

Knock! Knock!
Who's there?
Ewe.
Ewe who?
Ewe look familiar to me.

I JUST CAN'T PLACE THE FACE!

KNOCK! KNOCK!
WHO'S THERE?
AARDVARK.
AARDVARK WHO?
AARDVARK A MILLION MILES FOR ONE OF YOUR SMILES.

KNOCK! KNOCK!
WHO'S THERE?
HARE.
HARE WHO?
HARE WE GO AGAIN.

Knock! Knock!
Who's there?
Robin.
Robin who?
Robin people is a felony crime.

• •

Knock! Knock!
Who's there?
I flounder.
I flounder who?
I flounder in the shoe department.

• •

Knock! Knock!
Who's there?
A lioness.
A lioness who?
A lioness king of beasts.

• •

Knock! Knock!
Who's there?
Kelp.
Kelp who?
Kelp me. I can't swim!

Knock! Knock!
Who's there?
Swarm.
Swarm who?
Swarm in here, open a window.

KNOCK! KNOCK!
WHO'S THERE?
HIVE.
HIVE WHO?
HIVE GOT A BONE TO PICK WITH YOU.

Knock! Knock!
Who's there?
Whale.
Whale who?
Whale stop pollution someday soon.

Knock! Knock!
Who's there?
Ether.
Ether who?
Ether bunnies deliver colored eggs.

KNOCK! KNOCK!
WHO'S THERE?
EARL LEE.
EARL LEE WHO?
EARL LEE BIRDS CATCH THE WORM.

Knock! Knock!
Who's there?
Poodle.
Poodle who?
Poodle little trust in a stranger.

CHAPTER **3**
Funny Folks

Knock! Knock!
Who's there?
Tillie.
Tillie who?
Tillie opens the door, I'm staying right here.

▲▲▲▲▲▲▲▲▲▲▲▲▲▲▲▲▲▲▲▲▲▲▲▲▲▲▲▲▲▲

KNOCK! KNOCK!
WHO'S THERE?
I, NOAH.
I, NOAH WHO?
I NOAH SECRET SO OPEN UP.

▼▼▼▼▼▼▼▼▼▼▼▼▼▼▼▼▼▼▼▼▼▼▼▼▼▼▼▼▼

Knock! Knock!
Who's there?
Bennett.
Bennett who?
Bennett rains it pours.

▼▼▼▼▼▼▼▼▼▼▼▼▼▼▼

Knock! Knock!
Who's there?
Attila.
Attila who?
Attila tell you to open the door, keep it closed.

Knock! Knock!
Who's there?
Reed.
Reed who?
Reed some books over summer vacation.

KNOCK! KNOCK!
WHO'S THERE?
SY.
SY WHO?
SY-BER SPACE.

Knock! Knock!
Who's there?
Mae.
Mae who?
Mae I sit next to you?

Knock! Knock!
Who's there?
Thelma.
Thelma who?
Thelma I won't be home for dinner.

Knock! Knock!
Who's there?
Jimmy.
Jimmy who?
Jimmy your lunch money!

KNOCK! KNOCK!
WHO'S THERE?
MADISON.
MADISON WHO?
MADISON IS GOOD TO TAKE WHEN
YOU'RE SICK.

Knock! Knock!
Who's there?
Hank.
Hank who?
Don't mention it.

Knock! Knock!
Who's there?
Warren.
Warren who?
Warren you in this same class
last year?

Knock! Knock!
Who's there?
Roland.
Roland who?
Roland! Roland! Roland on a river.

Knock! Knock!
Who's there?
Cord.
Cord who?
Cord you please speak a little louder?

KNOCK! KNOCK!
WHO'S THERE?
STAN STELL.
STAN STELL WHO?
STAN STELL AND
STOP FIDGETING.

KNOCK! KNOCK!
WHO'S THERE?
FITZ.
FITZ WHO?
FITZ THE DOORBELL AND I
WON'T HAVE TO KNOCK.

Knock! Knock!
Who's there?
Aaron.
Aaron who?
Aaron away from home and now I miss my folks.

Knock! Knock!
Who's there?
Albie.
Albie who?
Albie a son of a gun.

Knock! Knock!
Who's there?
Checker.
Checker who?
Checker ID at the door.

Knock! Knock!
Who's there?
Norma Lee.
Norma Lee who?
Norma Lee I don't knock on the doors of strangers.

Knock! Knock!
Who's there?
Bill Clinton.
Bill Clinton who?
Bill Clinton for
the clothes Hillary
bought.

* * * * * * * * * * * * * * * * *

KNOCK! KNOCK!

WHO'S THERE?

WYATT.

WYATT WHO?

WYATT'S MY OLD PAL MORGAN.

Knock! Knock!
Who's there?
Effie.
Effie who?
Effie keeps knocking, call
the police.

Knock! Knock!
Who's there?
Thames.
Thames who?
Thames fightin' words, Englishman!

Knock! Knock!
Who's there?
Dozen.
Dozen who?
Dozen anyone care that I'm out here?

KNOCK! KNOCK!
WHO'S THERE?
ANN DAN.
ANN DAN WHO?
ANN DAN ALONG CAME JONES.

Knock! Knock!
Who's there?
Lars.
Lars who?
Lars tells a lot of fibs.

Knock! Knock!
Who's there?
Omar.
Omar who?
Omar goodness! I'm locked out.

KNOCK! KNOCK!
WHO'S THERE?
ANDY GREEN.
ANDY GREEN, WHO?
ANDY GREEN GRASS GROWS ALL AROUND,
ALL AROUND.

• •

Knock! Knock!
Who's there?
Harley.
Harley who?
Harley a day goes by when this
doesn't happen to me.

• •

Knock! Knock!
Who's there?
Howell.
Howell who?
Howell I get in if you don't open up?

• •

Knock! Knock!
Who's there?
Bertha.
Bertha who?
Bertha day greetings to you.

KNOCK! KNOCK!
WHO'S THERE?
ESTHER.
ESTHER WHO?
ESTHER ANOTHER DOOR I CAN GO TO?

Knock! Knock!
Who's there?
Manny.
Manny who?
Manny people know me and like me.

Knock! Knock!
Who's there?
Ann April.
Ann April who?
Ann April pound on his chest and break down your door.

Knock! Knock!
Who's there?
Avery.
Avery who?
Avery time I come here it's the same old thing.

Knock! Knock!
Who's there?
A.C.
A.C. who?
A.C. come A.C. go.

KNOCK! KNOCK!
WHO'S THERE?
ALMA.
ALMA WHO?
ALMA FRIENDS ARE OUT HERE TOO.

Knock! Knock!
Who's there?
Argo.
Argo who?
Argo jump in a lake.

Knock! Knock!
Who's there?
Alp.
Alp who?
Alp! Alp! I'm drowning.

KNOCK! KNOCK!
WHO'S THERE?
LURIE.
LURIE WHO?
LURIE LURIE HALLELUJAH.

Knock! Knock!
Who's there?
Albee.
Albee who?
Albee back tomorrow.

Knock! Knock!
Who's there?
Alda.
Alda who?
Alda neighbors let me in their houses.

Knock! Knock!
Who's there?
I Astor.
I Astor who?
I Astor very politely to open the door.

Knock! Knock!
Who's there?
Roland.
Roland who?
Roland down a hill will make you dizzy.

****

KNOCK! KNOCK!
WHO'S THERE?
ALEX.
ALEX WHO?
ALEX YOU ONE MORE TIME TO OPEN UP.

Knock! Knock!
Who's there?
Balfour.
Balfour who?
Balfour batter. Take your base.

Knock! Knock!
Who's there?
Stan Bach.
Stan Bach who?
Stan Bach! I'm breaking down the door.

KNOCK! KNOCK!
WHO'S THERE?
VENICE.
VENICE WHO?
VENICE PAYDAY? I'M
FLAT BROKE.

Knock! Knock!
Who's there?
It's Cole.
It's Cole who?
It's Cole out here. Let me come in.

****

Knock! Knock!
Who's there?
Hiram.
Hiram who?
Hiram because he's the right man
for the job.

Knock! Knock!
Who's there?
Guido.
Guido who?
Guidon't want anymore excuses. Open the door.

Knock! Knock!
Who's there?
Kay Jen.
Kay Jen who?
Kay Jen music has a peppy beat.

KNOCK! KNOCK!
WHO'S THERE?
I MIDAS.
I MIDAS WHO?
I MIDAS WELL GO HOME.

Knock! Knock!
Who's there?
Hugh Otto.
Hugh Otto who?
Hugh Otto know. You invited me over.

Knock! Knock!
Who's there?
Toodle.
Toodle who?
Right. See you later.

KNOCK! KNOCK!
WHO'S THERE?
TOM SAWYER.
TOM SAWYER WHO?
TOM SAWYER
SNEAKING OUT THE
BACK DOOR.

Knock! Knock!
Who's there?
Tamara.
Tamara who?
Tamara is another school day. Yuk!

Knock! Knock!
Who's there?
Gretta.
Gretta who?
Gretta long little doggie. Gretta long.

Knock! Knock!
Who's there?
Bay B.
Bay B. who
Bay B. Face Nelson.

Knock! Knock!
Who's there?
Ellison.
Ellison who?
Ellison the alphabet after K and before M.

• •

KNOCK! KNOCK!
WHO'S THERE?
MICHELLE.
MICHELLE WHO?
MICHELLE IS CRACKED, SAID THE TURTLE SADLY.

• •

Knock! Knock!
Who's there?
I'm Gibbon.
I'm Gibbon who?
I'm Gibbon away
free samples.

• • • • • • • • • •

Knock! Knock!
Who's there?
Watson.
Watson who?
Watson your mind, young fella?

KNOCK! KNOCK!
WHO'S THERE?
BOLIVAR.
BOLIVAR WHO?
BOLIVAR FRIENDS ARE ON THEIR
WAY OVER HERE.

• •

Knock! Knock!
Who's there?
Heidi.
Heidi who?
Heidi Ho everybody!

• •

Knock! Knock!
Who's there?
Abbott.
Abbott who?
Abbott you're afraid to open the door.

• •

KNOCK! KNOCK!
WHO'S THERE?
BARRIE.
BARRIE WHO?
BARRIE INTERESTING.

Knock! Knock!
Who's there?
Tara.
Tara who?
Tara-rah-boom-de yah!

KNOCK! KNOCK!
WHO'S THERE?
CAIN.
CAIN WHO?
CAIN I PLEASE COME IN?

* * * * * * * * * * * * * * * * *

Knock! Knock!
Who's there?
My Carlos.
My Carlos who?
My Carlos a wheel. I need help.

Knock! Knock!
Who's there?
Clare.
Clare who?
Clare a path! I'm coming through.

* *

KNOCK! KNOCK!
WHO'S THERE?
FOR BRYAN.
FOR BRYAN WHO?
FOR BRYAN OUT LOUD, OPEN UP.

* * * * * * * * * * * * * * * * * * *

Knock! Knock!
Who's there?
Shelby.
Shelby who?
Shelby right with you, so be patient.

Knock! Knock!
Who's there?
Ray.
Ray who?
No. Who Ray! It's me.

* *

Knock! Knock!
Who's there?
Carmen.
Carmen who?
Carmen get it. I have hot pizza.

Knock! Knock!
Who's there?
Amos.
Amos who?
Amos stop coming to this house.

Knock! Knock!
Who's there?
Luke.
Luke who?
Luke and see you dummy!

Knock! Knock!
Who's there?
Cheryl B.
Cheryl B. who?
Cheryl B. coming around the mountain when she comes.

KNOCK! KNOCK!
WHO'S THERE?
I'M SUE.
I'M SUE WHO?
I'M SUE SORRY TO BE LATE.

Knock! Knock!
Who's there?
Rein.
Rein who?
Rein Irish eyes are smiling.

▼▼▼▼▼▼▼▼▼▼▼▼▼▼▼▼▼▼▼▼▼▼▼▼▼▼▼▼▼▼

Knock! Knock!
Who's there?
Omar.
Omar who?
Omar Darling Clementine.

▲▲▲▲▲▲▲▲▲▲▲▲▲▲▲▲▲▲▲▲▲▲▲▲▲▲▲▲▲▲

Knock! Knock!
Who's there?
Will Lama.
Will Lama who?
Will Lama monkey's uncle!

▼▼▼▼▼▼▼▼▼▼▼▼▼▼▼▼▼▼▼▼▼▼▼▼▼▼▼▼▼▼

Knock! Knock!
Who's there?
Hugo.
Hugo who?
Hugo first. I'll follow.

Knock! Knock!
Who's there?
Sharon.
Sharon who?
Sharon gossip is fun. Have you heard this rumor?

Knock! Knock!
Who's there?
Ray.
Ray who?
Ray to go dude.

Knock! Knock!
Who's there?
Butch.
Butch who?
Butch your arms around me
and give me a big hug.

Knock! Knock!
Who's there?
Alfred.
Alfred who?
Alfred the needle if you sew
up the rip.

KNOCK! KNOCK!
WHO'S THERE?
GUS.
GUS WHO?
THAT'S WHAT YOU HAVE TO DO. GUESS.

Knock! Knock!
Who's there?
Danielle.
Danielle who?
Danielle at me. Speak softly.

KNOCK! KNOCK!
WHO'S THERE?
DALE.
DALE WHO?
DALE BE HECK TO PAY IF YOU DON'T LET ME IN.

Knock! Knock!
Who's there?
Hiam.
Hiam who?
Hiam here on police business.
Open up!

Knock! Knock!
Who's there?
Elf S.
Elf S. who?
Elf S. Presley.

* * * * * * * * *

Knock! Knock!
Who's there?
Hardy.
Hardy who?
Hardy har har! The joke is over. Let us in.

* *

KNOCK! KNOCK!
WHO'S THERE?
NOBEL.
NOBEL WHO?
NOBEL SO I KNOCKED INSTEAD.

Knock! Knock!
Who's there?
Dee.
Dee who?
Dee heck with you! I'm leaving.

Knock! Knock!
Who's there?
Ali.
Ali who?
Ali bama is a fine state.

KNOCK! KNOCK!
WHO'S THERE?
BRUNO.
BRUNO WHO?
BRUNO ME. I LIVE NEXT DOOR.

* *

Knock! Knock!
Who's there?
Burton.
Burton who?
Burton up your coat.
It's cold outside.

Knock! Knock!
Who's there?
Wilda.
Wilda who?
Wilda plane be landing soon?

Knock! Knock!
Who's there?
Olive.
Olive who?
Olive the springtime, don't you.

KNOCK! KNOCK!
WHO'S THERE?
JESTER.
JESTER WHO?
JESTER MINUTE. I'M
STILL THINKING.

Knock! Knock!
Who's there?
Skip.
Skip who?
Skip it! I'll go next door.

Knock! Knock!
Who's there?
Kent.
Kent who?
Kent you see who I am?

KNOCK! KNOCK!
WHO'S THERE?
OTTO.
OTTO WHO?
OTTO KNOW.

Knock! Knock!
Who's there?
Juno.
Juno who?
Juno how long I've been waiting out here?

Knock! Knock!
Who's there?
Howard.
Howard who?
Howard you like to buy some magazines?

Knock! Knock!
Who's there?
Ernie.
Ernie who?
Ernie got scraped when she fell on the sidewalk.

Knock! Knock!
Who's there?
Wilder.
Wilder who?
Wilder out let's order pizza.

• •

Knock! Knock!
Who's there?
Ozzie.
Ozzie who?
Ozzie a bad moon rising.

• •

KNOCK! KNOCK!
WHO'S THERE?
OSBORNE.
OSBORNE WHO?
OSBORNE ON THE 4TH OF JULY.

• •

KNOCK! KNOCK!
WHO'S THERE?
WINNIE.
WINNIE WHO?
WINNIE GETS HOME, HE'S IN FOR A BIG SURPRISE.

Knock! Knock!
Who's there?
Hubie.
Hubie who?
Hubie a good boy while we're gone!

Knock! Knock!
Who's there?
Al.
Al who?
Al in favor, say aye!

Knock! Knock!
Who's there?
Len.
Len who?
**Len me ten bucks
until payday.**

KnockKnock!
Who's there?
Althea.
Althea who?
Althea later, dude.

Knock! Knock!
Who's there?
Megan.
Megan who?
Megan dinner is a lot of work.

****

Knock! Knock!
Who's there?
Lexie.
Lexie who?
Lexie how long you'll keep me waiting.

Knock! Knock!
Who's there?
Jamaica.
Jamaica who?
Jamaica a snack for us?

KNOCK! KNOCK!
WHO'S THERE?
HYGIENE.
HYGIENE WHO?
HYGIENE! WHAT'S NEW WITH YOU, GENE?

Knock! Knock!
Who's there?
Marcella.
Marcella who?
Marcella is flooded. Can I borrow a mop?

Knock! Knock!
Who's there?
Mo.
Mo who?
Mo lasses is very
sweet syrup.

KNOCK! KNOCK!
WHO'S THERE?
GWEN.
GWEN WHO?
GWEN ARE YOU GOING TO OPEN THIS
DARN DOOR?

Knock! Knock!
Who's there?
I'm Shad.
I'm Shad who?
I'm Shad to see you go.

Knock! Knock!
Who's there?
Gandhi.
Gandhi who?
Gandhi kids come out to play?

▲▲▲▲▲▲▲▲▲▲▲▲▲▲▲▲▲▲▲▲▲▲▲▲▲▲▲▲

Knock! Knock!
Who's there?
Will Hugh?
Will Hugh who?
Will Hugh
marry me?

▼▼▼▼▼▼▼▼▼▼▼▼▼▼▼▼▼▼▼▼▼▼▼▼▼▼▼▼▼▼

CHAPTER
4
Jokey Jobs

Knock! Knock!
Who's there?
Olive.
Olive who?
Olive our job openings are filled.

Knock! Knock!
Who's there?
Alana.
Alana who?
Alana Georgia is where my
factory is located.

KNOCK! KNOCK!
WHO'S THERE?
MYSTERY.
MYSTERY WHO?
MYSTERY ARGUE OVER YOUR BONUS.

Knock! Knock!
Who's there?
Toupee.
Toupee who?
Toupee my bills, I had to
borrow money.

Knock! Knock!
Who's there?
I Cher.
I Cher who?
I Cher would like to work here.

KNOCK! KNOCK!
WHO'S THERE?
DARYL.
DARYL WHO?
DARYL BE A BONUS IN THIS DEAL FOR YOU.

Knock! Knock!
Who's there?
Foreman.
Foreman who?
Foreman get more work
done than three men.
* * * * * * * * * * *

WE CAN'T ALL BE IN CHARGE OF THIS JOB!

Knock! Knock!
Who's there?
Euell.
Euell who?
Euell be sorry if you don't hire me.

Knock! Knock!
Who's there?
Dakota.
Dakota who?
Dakota paint you put on my house is starting to peel.

Knock! Knock!
Who's there?
Event.
Event who?
Event home sick from work.

Knock! Knock!
Who's there?
Sofa.
Sofa who?
Sofa we have two good applicants for the job.

KNOCK! KNOCK!
WHO'S THERE?
A BONUS.
A BONUS WHO?
A BONUS WHAT A DOG LIKES TO CHEW.

Knock! Knock!
Who's there?
Abby.
Abby who?
Abby up for parole soon.

• •

Knock! Knock!
Who's there?
Denny.
Denny who?
Denny took the money and ran.

• •

KNOCK! KNOCK!
WHO'S THERE?
THE PARSON.
THE PARSON WHO?
THE PARSON I SAW COMMIT THE CRIME
IS GETTING AWAY.

• •

Knock! Knock!
Who's there?
Phew.
Phew who?
Phew have the right to an attorney.

Knock! Knock!
Who's there?
Eye.
Eye who?
Eye swear to tell the whole truth, judge.

* * * * * * * * *

Knock! Knock!
Who's there?
Invest.
Invest who?
Invest-igate all of the suspects.

Knock! Knock!
Who's there?
Hiam.
Hiam who?
Hiam totally innocent.

Knock! Knock!
Who's there?
Year.
Year who?
Year honor is being unfair to my client.

Knock! Knock!
Who's there?
Tess.
Tess who?
Tess-tify as to what you saw.

KNOCK! KNOCK!
WHO'S THERE?
ENOS.
ENOS WHO?
ENOS I'M NOT GUILTY.

Knock! Knock!
Who's there?
Aye, Aye.
Aye, Aye who?
Aye, Aye was robbed, robbed.

KNOCK! KNOCK!
WHO'S THERE?
DEBBY.
DEBBY WHO?
DEBBY NO CHARGE FOR
YOUR PHYSICAL EXAM.

Knock! Knock!
Who's there?
Shirley.
Shirley who?
Shirley you must know what's wrong with me.

* * * * * * * * * * * * * * * * * * * *

KNOCK! KNOCK!
WHO'S THERE?
CARRIE.
CARRIE WHO?
CARRIE ON SERGEANT.

* * * * * * * * * * * * * * * * * * *

Knock! Knock!
Who's there?
Haul.
Haul who?
Haul hands on deck.

* *

Knock! Knock!
Who's there?
Zeke.
Zeke who?
Zeke out and destroy all enemy outposts.

Knock! Knock!
Who's there?
Ann.
Ann who?
Ann-chors away, my boys.

* * * * * * * * * * * * * * * * * *

Knock! Knock!
Who's there?
Huff.
Huff who?
Huff we go into the wild blue yonder.

* * * * * * * * * * * * * * * * * *

KNOCK! KNOCK!
WHO'S THERE?
TOUR.
TOUR WHO?
TOUR-PEDOES ARE FIRED FROM SUBMARINES.

* * * * * * * * * * * * * * * * * * *

Knock! Knock!
Who's there?
Toucan.
Toucan who?
Toucan no longer live as
cheaply as one.

Knock! Knock!
Who's there?
Refund.
Refund who?
Refund two charity events every year.

Knock! Knock!
Who's there?
Account.
Account who?
Account is just as important as a duke or a baron.

KNOCK! KNOCK!
WHO'S THERE?
EEL.
EEL WHO?
EEL SHOW YOU WHERE THE SALE ITEMS ARE.

Knock! Knock!
Who's there?
Seldom.
Seldom who?
Seldom some common stock.

Knock! Knock!
Who's there?
I Rhoda.
I Rhoda who?
I Rhoda book and I hope it becomes a bestseller.

• •

KNOCK! KNOCK!

WHO'S THERE?

G.I.

G.I. WHO?

G.I DON'T REMEMBER MY OWN NAME.

I THINK IT RHYMES WITH "SCHMOE".

CHAPTER **5**

Punny Places

Knock! Knock!
Who's there?
Iran.
Iran who?
Iran all the way home from school today.

▲▲▲▲▲▲▲▲▲▲▲▲▲▲▲▲▲▲▲▲▲▲▲▲▲▲▲▲▲▲▲

Knock! Knock!
Who's there?
Sahara.
Sahara who?
Sahara you today?

▼▼▼▼▼▼▼▼▼▼▼▼▼▼▼▼▼▼▼▼▼▼▼▼▼▼▼▼▼▼▼

Knock! Knock!
Who's there?
Asia.
Asia who?
Asia mother home from work yet?

KNOCK! KNOCK!
WHO'S THERE?
RIO.
RIO WHO?
RIO FUNNY WISE-GUY, YOU KNOW IT'S ME.

Knock! Knock!
Who's there?
Tibet.
Tibet who?
Tibet is to risk losing your money.

● ● ● ● ● ● ● ● ●

Knock! Knock!
Who's there?
Knoxville.
Knoxville who?
Knoxville get an answer eventually.

KNOCK! KNOCK!
WHO'S THERE?
ANNAPOLIS.
ANNAPOLIS WHO?
ANNAPOLIS IS A TASTY FRUIT.

Knock! Knock!
Who's there?
Alaska.
Alaska who?
Alaska very nicely to open the door.

Knock! Knock!
Who's there?
Oz.
Oz who?
Oz tired of this knocking routine.

Knock! Knock!
Who's there?
Jupiter.
Jupiter who?
Jupiter a cracker in my soup?

KNOCK! KNOCK!
WHO'S THERE?
AURORA.
AURORA WHO?
AURORA BOREALIS.

Knock! Knock!
Who's there?
Japan.
Japan who?
Japan my trampoline and bounce around.

KNOCK! KNOCK!
WHO'S THERE?
RALEIGH.
RALEIGH WHO?
RALEIGH GOES FOR HELP,
LET'S GET ACQUAINTED.

Knock! Knock!
Who's there?
Hades.
Hades who?
Hades and gentlemen and children
of all ages.

Knock! Knock!
Who's there?
Cyprus.
Cyprus who?
Cyprus the doorbell and
press it hard.

KNOCK! KNOCK!
WHO'S THERE?
TAIWAN.
TAIWAN WHO?
TAIWAN SHOE AND LEAVE THE OTHER UNTIED.

Knock! Knock!
Who's there?
Europe.
Europe who?
Europe early this morning.

Knock! Knock!
Who's there?
Polynesia.
Polynesia who?
Polynesia cracker.

Knock! Knock!
Who's there?
Texas.
Texas who?
Texas the answer.

DON'T THINK OF IT AS A HANDOUT...

KNOCK! KNOCK!
WHO'S THERE?
NEVER NEVER LAND
NEVER NEVER LAND WHO?
NEVER NEVER LAND
MONEY TO A STRANGER.

Knock! Knock!
Who's there?
Formosa.
Formosa who?
Formosa the day I just goofed off.

* * * * * * * * * * * * * * * * * *

KNOCK! KNOCK!
WHO'S THERE?
EDEN.
EDEN WHO?
EDEN TOO MUCH WILL MAKE YOU GAIN WEIGHT.

Knock! Knock!
Who's there?
New Haven.
New Haven who?
New Haven any fun in there?

* * * * * * * * * * * * * * * * * * * *

Knock! Knock!
Who's there?
Catskill.
Catskill who?
Catskill mice.

KNOCK! KNOCK!
WHO'S THERE?
RUSSIA.
RUSSIA WHO?
RUSSIA OUT OF THERE, SHE'S LATE.

Knock! Knock!
Who's there?
Be in Cheyenne.
Be in Cheyenne who?
Be in Cheyenne bashful can
make people nervous.

Knock! Knock!
Who's there?
Idaho.
Idaho who?
Idaho sub sandwich for lunch, but I'm hungry again.

* *

Knock! Knock!
Who's there?
Utah.
Utah who?
Utah what she did to me, didn't you?

Knock! Knock!
Who's there?
Macon.
Macon who?
Macon friends in a new town
can be difficult.

* * * * * * * * * * * * * * * * * * *

KNOCK! KNOCK!
WHO'S THERE?
VENICE.
VENICE WHO?
VENICE HOT OUTSIDE, I GO SWIMMING.

* * * * * * * * * * * * * * * * * * *

Knock! Knock!
Who's there?
Isle.
Isle who?
Isle swat that pesky fly yet.

* * * * * * * * * * * * * * * * * * *

Knock! Knock!
Who's there?
Cairo.
Cairo who?
Cairo the boat now?

CHAPTER ✳✳6✳✳
Sports Snickers

Knock! Knock!
Who's there?
I Opie.
I Opie who?
I Opie makes a hole in one.

KNOCK! KNOCK!
WHO'S THERE?
HUMUS.
HUMUS WHO?
HUMUS GET A HIT OR WE'LL
LOSE THE GAME.

Knock! Knock!
Who's there?
Yule.
Yule who?
Yule be a good player if
you practice a lot.

Knock! Knock!
Who's there?
Juicy.
Juicy who?
Juicy that fantastic double play?

KNOCK! KNOCK!
WHO'S THERE?
NOAH.
NOAH WHO?
NOAH DIDN'T HIT MY OPPONENT
BELOW THE BELT.

Knock! Knock!
Who's there?
Hugo.
Hugo who?
Hugo downfield and out and I'll
pass you the football.

Knock! Knock!
Who's there?
Tumor.
Tumor who?
Tumor short runs and we'll punt the ball.

Knock! Knock!
Who's there?
Phyllis.
Phyllis who?
Phyllis in on all the latest scores.

Knock! Knock!
Who's there?
Recall.
Recall who?
Recall the plays the way we see them.

KNOCK! KNOCK!
WHO'S THERE?
ISLE.
ISLE WHO?
ISLE LET YOU PLAY FIRST BASE
NEXT INNING.

Knock! Knock!
Who's there?
Ida.
Ida who?
Ida wanna play right field, coach.

Knock! Knock!
Who's there?
Atlas.
Atlas who?
Atlas we meet for the heavyweight boxing title.

KNOCK! KNOCK!
WHO'S THERE?
DISSENTER.
DISSENTER WHO?
DISSENTER FIELDER CATCHES A LOT
OF FLY BALLS.

Knock! Knock!
Who's there?
Wail.
Wail who?
Wail pitch around this batter to get to the next hitter.

Knock! Knock!
Who's there?
Wayne.
Wayne who?
Wayne delays are common
in baseball.

Knock! Knock!
Who's there?
Dozen.
Dozen who?
Dozen he know three
strikes and he's out?

STRIKE TWELVE!

Knock! Knock!
Who's there?
Howie.
Howie who?
Howie getting into the stadium without tickets?

✳ ✳

Knock! Knock!
Who's there?
Europe.
Europe who?
Europe at bat next so get ready.

Knock! Knock!
Who's there?
Tijuana.
Tijuana who?
Tijuana place some one-on-one?

Knock! Knock!
Who's there?
Alice.
Alice who?
Alice our clean-up hitter.

KNOCK! KNOCK!
WHO'S THERE?
AVERY.
AVERY WHO?
AVERY TIME I SWING AT BAD PITCHES,
I STRIKE OUT.

Knock! Knock!
Who's there?
Willie.
Willie who?
Willie pass the ball or run it.

Knock! Knock!
Who's there?
Canoe.
Canoe who?
Canoe give me some batting tips?

KNOCK! KNOCK!
WHO'S THERE?
ARAB.
ARAB WHO?
ARAB MY PITCHING
ARM WHEN IT FEELS
SORE.

Knock! Knock!
Who's there?
Pitcher.
Pitcher who?
Pitcher hand on the doorknob
and open the door.

* * * * * * * * * * * * * * * * * * *

Knock! Knock!
Who's there?
Adolf.
Adolf who?
Adolf ball hit me in da mouf.

* * * * * * * * * * * * * * * * * * *

Knock! Knock!
Who's there?
Rush Hour.
Rush Hour who?
Rush Hour quarterback and
we'll block you.

* * * * * * * * * * * * * * * * * * *

CHAPTER

7

Open the Door Already!

Knock! Knock!
Who's there?
Heywood, Hugh, Harry.
Heywood, Hugh, Harry who?
Heywood, Hugh, Harry up and
open the door.

****

KNOCK! KNOCK!

WHO'S THERE?

WYLIE'S.

WYLIE'S WHO?

WYLIE'S LOOKING THE OTHER WAY, OPEN UP.

Knock! Knock!
Who's there?
Whys.
Whys who?
Whys up and open the door.

Knock! Knock!
Who's there?
Gas.
Gas who?
No. You gas who this is.

KNOCK! KNOCK!
WHO'S THERE?
CHESTER.
CHESTER WHO?
CHESTER ORDINARY DOOR-TO-DOOR SALESMAN.

****

Knock! Knock!
Who's there?
Hildegard.
Hildegard who?
Hildegard the door!

Knock! Knock!
Who's there?
Comb.
Comb who?
Comb out and play with me.

Knock! Knock!
Who's there?
Alibi.
Alibi who?
Alibi you a box of candy if you
open the door.

Knock! Knock!
Who's there?
Witch.
Witch who?
Witch part of open up do you not understand?

· ·

Knock! Knock!
Who's there?
Tea.
Tea who?
Tea if you can guess who I am.

IF IT ISN'T MY OLD FRIEND EARL GREY!

· ·

Knock! Knock!
Who's there?
Wool.
Wool who?
Wool you open up?

· ·

Knock! Knock!
Who's there?
Roulette.
Roulette who?
Roulette us in this instant!

KNOCK! KNOCK!
WHO'S THERE?
I LLOYD.
I LLOYD WHO?
I LLOYD WHEN I SAID I WAS LEAVING.

Knock! Knock!
Who's there?
Emma Dunn.
Emma Dunn who?
Emma Dunn playing games. Open up!

Knock! Knock!
Who's there?
Dulcy.
Dulcy who?
Dulcy who is at the back door.

KNOCK! KNOCK!
WHO'S THERE?
COMMA.
COMMA WHO?
COMMA LITTLE CLOSER TO THE DOOR.

Knock! Knock!
Who's there?
Henny.
Henny who?
Henny body home?

Knock! Knock!
Who's there?
Thesis.
Thesis who?
Thesis a stickup!

KNOCK! KNOCK!
WHO'S THERE?
OBSCENE.
OBSCENE WHO?
OBSCENE YOU OPEN THIS DOOR BEFORE.

KNOCK! KNOCK!
WHO'S THERE?
HANDY.
HANDY WHO?
HANDY KEY FOOD THROUGH THE MAIL SLOT.

Knock! Knock!
Who's there?
Hugh Juan.
Hugh Juan who?
Hugh Juan a prize. Open the door.

Knock! Knock!
Who's there?
Evonne.
Evonne who?
Evonne though I'm mad, I still want to come in.

Knock! Knock!
Who's there?
Dawn.
Dawn who?
Dawn you like surprise visitors?

Knock! Knock!
Who's there?
Enid.
Enid who?
Enid a shame the way you lock me out?

Knock! Knock!
Who's there?
Far.
Far who?
Far the love of Pete, open up!

* * * * * * * * * * * * * * * * * * *

Knock! Knock!
Who's there?
Soda.
Soda who?
Soda answer is still no admittance?

* * * * * * * * * * * * * * * * *

Knock! Knock!
Who's there?
Lena.
Lena who?
Lena over and look through the mail slot.

* * * * * * * * * * * * * * * * * * *

KNOCK! KNOCK!
WHO'S THERE?
OTTO.
OTTO WHO?
OTTO MY WAY! I'M COMING IN.

Knock! Knock!
Who's there?
Marque.
Marque who?
Marque doesn't work, so unlock
the door.

****

Knock! Knock!
Who's there?
Omar.
Omar who?
Omar goodness. I came to the
wrong house.

KNOCK! KNOCK!
WHO'S THERE?
VILLA.
VILLA WHO?
VILLA YOU OPEN THE DOOR OR NOT?

Knock! Knock!
Who's there?
Taylor.
Taylor who?
Taylor to open this door right now.

Knock! Knock!
Who's there?
Abby.
Abby who?
Abby back tomorrow if you
don't open up now.

Knock! Knock!
Who's there?
Effie.
Effie who?
Effie wants me to, I'll come back later.

KNOCK! KNOCK!
WHO'S THERE?
AUNT TILLIE.
AUNT TILLIE WHO?
AUNT TILLIE SAYS COME IN,
I'M STAYING RIGHT HERE.

Knock! Knock!
Who's there?
Poker.
Poker who?
Poker in the eye if she looks
through the peephole.

Knock! Knock!
Who's there?
Axe.
Axe who?
Axe your mom if she wants
to buy some magazines.

● ●

KNOCK! KNOCK!
WHO'S THERE?
GRANITE.
GRANITE WHO?
GRANITE I'M A BIT EARLY, BUT WILL YOU
PLEASE OPEN UP?

● ●

Knock! Knock!
Who's there?
Isadore.
Isadore who?
Isadore locked and bolted?

● ●

Minnie: Knock! Knock!
Binnie: Who's there?
Minnie: A person too short to reach
the doorbell.

Knock! Knock!
Who's there?
Vet.
Vet who?
Vet you tink you doing in dere? Open up.

Knock! Knock!
Who's there?
Gino.
Gino who?
Gino who this is?

KNOCK! KNOCK!
WHO'S THERE?
HANNAH.
HANNAH WHO?
HANNAH OVER THE KEY.

Knock! Knock!
Who's there?
Annie.
Annie who?
Annie of my friends in there?

Knock! Knock!
Who's there?
Aloe.
Aloe who?
Aloe in there. Is anybody home?

Knock! Knock!
Who's there?
Dale.
Dale who?
Dale be trouble if you don't open up.

Knock! Knock!
Who's there?
Hale.
Hale who?
Hale! Hale! The gang's all here!

KNOCK! KNOCK!
WHO'S THERE?
GILLETTE.
GILLETTE WHO?
GILLETTE MY DOG COME IN?

KNOCK! KNOCK!
WHO'S THERE?
GOLDIE.
GOLDIE WHO?
GOLDIE LOCKS THE DOOR TOO.

Knock! Knock!
Who's there?
Nicolet.
Nicolet who?
Nicolet me in, won't he?

* *

Knock! Knock!
Who's there?
Schooner.
Schooner who?
Schooner or later
you'll open the door.

AHOY!

* * * * * * * * * *

Knock! Knock!
Who's there?
Henry.
Henry who?
Henry come in now?

Knock! Knock!
Who's there?
Whiskey.
Whiskey who?
Whiskey opens this locked door?

- -

KNOCK! KNOCK!
WHO'S THERE?
WILMA.
WILMA WHO?
WILMA HAND FALL OFF IF I KEEP KNOCKING?

****

Knock! Knock!
Who's there?
Pressure.
Pressure who?
Pressure ear to the door and I'll whisper my name.

Knock! Knock!
Who's there?
Oral.
Oral who?
Oral stop knocking if you'll open up.

Knock! Knock!
Who's there?
Wooden shoe.
Wooden shoe who?
Wooden shoe like to let me in?

Knock! Knock!
Who's there?
Ham Bacon.
Ham Bacon who?
Ham Bacon you
to let me in.

Knock! Knock!
Who's there?
Yoda.
Yoda who?
Yoda man, so open
up bro!

KNOCK! KNOCK!
WHO'S THERE?
DON HUGH.
DON HUGH WHO?
DON HUGH KNOW WHO I AM?

Knock! Knock!
Who's there?
Cayuse.
Cayuse who?
Cayuse the restroom?

KNOCK! KNOCK!
WHO'S THERE?
I'M GLADYS.
I'M GLADYS WHO?
I'M GLADYS YOU. ARE YOU GLADYS ME?

Knock! Knock!
Who's there?
Apollo.
Apollo who?
Apollo all your instructions if you open the door.

Knock! Knock!
Who's there?
Vera.
Vera who?
Vera you hiding?

Knock! Knock!
Who's there?
Stalin.
Stalin who?
Stalin me won't work.
Open up!

Knock! Knock!
Who's there?
Knox.
Knox who?
Knox don't work. Let's try the doorbell.

Knock! Knock!
Who's there?
Habit.
Habit who?
Habit you're afraid to open the door.

Knock! Knock!
Who's there?
Closure.
Closure who?
Closure mouth and open the door.

KNOCK! KNOCK!
WHO'S THERE?
AUSSIE.
AUSSIE WHO?
AUSSIE YOU TOMORROW, MATE.

Knock! Knock!
Who's there?
Forgots.
Forgots who?
Forgots sake open up! I need help.

KNOCK! KNOCK!
WHO'S THERE?
IRELAND.
IRELAND WHO?
IRELAND YOU FIVE BUCKS IF YOU
PROMISE TO OPEN THE DOOR.

Knock! Knock!
Who's there?
Whirl.
Whirl who?
Whirl try again later.

Knock! Knock!
Who's there?
Hiss.
Hiss who?
Hiss anyone else home besides you?

* * * * * * * * * * * * * * * * * * * *

Knock! Knock!
Who's there?
Hyphen.
Hyphen who?
Hyphen waiting out here a long time.

KNOCK! KNOCK!
WHO'S THERE?
OIL.
OIL WHO?
OIL SEE YOU LATER.

* *

Knock! Knock!
Who's there?
Adore.
Adore who?
Adore is between us. Open up.

Knock! Knock!
Who's there?
Habit.
Habit who?
Habit your way, I'll come
back later.

* * * * * * * *

KNOCK! KNOCK!
WHO'S THERE?
DISGUISE.
DISGUISE WHO?
DISGUISE GETTING
VERY IMPATIENT.

* * * * * * * * * *

DON'T MAKE ME WAIT OUT HERE FOREVER!

Knock! Knock!
Who's there?
Radio.
Radio who?
Radio not. Here I come.

Knock! Knock!
Who's there?
Allied.
Allied who?
Allied when I said I'm not mad. Open up!

Knock! Knock!
Who's there?
Musk.
Musk who?
Musk I knock again?

• •

KNOCK! KNOCK!
WHO'S THERE?
HALO.
HALO WHO?
HALO AND GOOD-BYE. I'M TIRED OF WAITING.

• •

Knock! Knock!
Who's there?
Poison Ally.
Poison Ally who?
Poison Ally I don't care
if you open up or not.

• •

Knock! Knock!
Who's there?
Ribbon.
Ribbon who?
Ribbon looking for your house for hours.

KNOCK! KNOCK!
WHO'S THERE?
HAROLD.
HAROLD WHO?
HAROLD DO YOU HAVE TO BE TO GET IN?

Knock! Knock!
Who's there?
Amin.
Amin who?
Amin you no harm. Open up.

Knock! Knock!
Who's there?
Spine.
Spine who?
Spine on me through the peephole is not very polite.

Knock! Knock!
Who's there?
Euclid.
Euclid who?
Euclid be more friendly to visitors.

Knock! Knock!
Who's there?
Beth.
Beth who?
Beth you don't know who this is!

Knock! Knock!
Who's there?
Wah.
Wah who?
Okay, I'm leaving. You don't have to get so excited.

CHAPTER
8*
Last Laughs

Knock! Knock!
Who's there?
Despair.
Despair who?
Despair of shoes is too tight.

Knock! Knock!
Who's there?
Beehive.
Beehive who?
Beehive when we get to Grandma's
house or you'll be sorry.
****

Knock! Knock!
Who's there?
Icy.
Icy who?
Icy you have a
satellite dish.
• • • • • • • • • •

KNOCK! KNOCK!
WHO'S THERE?
RAIL.
RAIL WHO?
RAIL BE HOME LATE, SO DON'T WAIT UP.

Knock! Knock!
Who's there?
Ardor.
Ardor who?
Ardor any chicken wings left?

****

Knock! Knock!
Who's there?
Teller.
Teller who?
Teller a good joke and she'll
laugh out loud.

KNOCK! KNOCK!
WHO'S THERE?
MUSK.
MUSK WHO?
MUSK YOU ALWAYS BE SO STUBBORN?

Knock! Knock!
Who's there?
I mist.
I mist who?
I mist you at the party last night.

Knock! Knock!
Who's there?
A vowel.
A vowel who?
A vowel-in-tine for you.

•••••••••••••••••••••••••

Knock! Knock!
Who's there?
Nickel.
Nickel who?
Nickel vouch for me. Just ask Nick.

•••••••••••••••••••••••••

KNOCK! KNOCK!
WHO'S THERE?
HOWDY.
HOWDY WHO?
HOWDY DO THAT?

•••••••••••••••••••••••••

KNOCK! KNOCK!
WHO'S THERE?
CHRISTMAS.
CHRISTMAS WHO?
CHRISTMAS BE LOST, CALL CHRIS
ON HIS CELL PHONE.

Knock! Knock!
Who's there?
Dare.
Dare who?
Dare must be some mistake.

Knock! Knock!
Who's there?
Huron.
Huron who?
Huron dangerous ground.

Knock! Knock!
Who's there?
Dairy.
Dairy who?
Dairy goes!
After him, men!

Knock! Knock!
Who's there?
Fiber.
Fiber who?
Fiber get you I'll try to remember you tomorrow.

KNOCK! KNOCK!
WHO'S THERE?
FAUN KNEE
FAUN KNEE WHO?
FAUN KNEE YOU SHOULD ASK
THAT QUESTION.

Knock! Knock!
Who's there?
Sedan.
Sedan who?
Sedan you're rocking the boat.

KNOCK! KNOCK!
WHO'S THERE?
ARCH.
ARCH WHO?
YOU'D BETTER TAKE SOMETHING FOR THAT COLD.

Knock! Knock!
Who's there?
Unaware.
Unaware who?
Unaware is what you put on
first when you get dressed.

Knock! Knock!
Who's there?
Teller.
Teller who?
Teller a good joke and make her laugh.

Knock! Knock!
Who's there?
Socket.
Socket who?
Socket to me.

Knock! Knock!
Who's there?
Somber.
Somber who?
Somber over the rainbow.

Knock! Knock!
Who's there?
Getty.
Getty who?
Getty yap horse, we're out of here.

Knock! Knock!
Who's there?
Mice.
Mice who?
Mice weather we're
having, isn't it?

* * * * * * * * *

Knock! Knock!
Who's there?
Market.
Market who?
Market C.O.D.

Knock! Knock!
Who's there?
Kleenex.
Kleenex who?
Kleenex are nicer than dirty necks.
* * * * * * * * * * * * * * * * * * *

Knock! Knock!
Who's there?
Butcher.
Butcher who?
Butcher money where your
mouth is, wise guy.

KNOCK! KNOCK!
WHO'S THERE?
COWL.
COWL WHO?
COWL GET EVEN WITH YOU FOR THIS.

* * * * * * * * * * * * * * * * * * * *

Knock! Knock!
Who's there?
Zoom.
Zoom who?
Zoom did you expect?

Knock! Knock!
Who's there?
Almond.
Almond who?
Almond a very good mood.

KNOCK! KNOCK!
WHO'S THERE?
Z.
Z WHO?
Z YOU IN THE MORNING.

Knock! Knock!
Who's there?
Rock it.
Rock it who?
Rock it ships fly into space.

Knock! Knock!
Who's there?
Canopy.
Canopy who?
Canopy ever grow up to be a string bean?

Knock! Knock!
Who's there?
Oil.
Oil who?
Oil paint your
picture if you'll
pose for me.

KNOCK! KNOCK!
WHO'S THERE?
DOT COM.
DOT COM WHO?
DOT COM HOME, WE DON'T MISS YOU.

Knock! Knock!
Who's there?
Freeze.
Freeze who?
Freeze a jolly good fellow,
which nobody can deny.

Knock! Knock!
Who's there?
Hour.
Hour who?
Hour you feeling? Better, I hope.

KNOCK! KNOCK!
WHO'S THERE?
VENICE.
VENICE WHO?
VENICE THE NEXT TRAIN TO ROME?

Knock! Knock!
Who's there?
Snow.
Snow who?
No. Snow what and the
Seven Dwarfs.

Knock! Knock!
Who's there?
Vicious.
Vicious who?
Vicious a fine howdy
do for a visitor.

Knock! Knock!
Who's there?
Data.
Data who?
Data nice boy.

Knock! Knock!
Who's there?
Kenya.
Kenya who?
Kenya kids come out to play?

Knock! Knock!
Who's there?
Rut.
Rut who?
Rut do you want me to say?

Knock! Knock!
Who's there?
Ride.
Ride who?
Ride you tell a fib about me?

KNOCK! KNOCK!
WHO'S THERE?
HILL.
HILL WHO?
HILL BE BACK AFTER LUNCH.

Knock! Knock!
Who's there?
Reveal.
Reveal who?
Reveal you deserve a promotion.

KNOCK! KNOCK!
WHO'S THERE?
WAGONS.
WAGONS WHO?
NO. IT'S WAGONS HO!

Knock! Knock!
Who's there?
Aisle.
Aisle who?
Aisle call you when I get to the mall.

****

KNOCK! KNOCK!
WHO'S THERE?
WEEVIL.
WEEVIL WHO?
WEEVIL HEARD ENOUGH ABOUT THE CIVIL WAR FOR ONE DAY.

Knock! Knock!
Who's there?
Water.
Water who?
Water you waiting for?
Get to class.

Knock! Knock!
Who's there?
Sum.
Sum who?
Sum math teachers are harder than others.

KNOCK! KNOCK!
WHO'S THERE?
GINO.
GINO WHO?
GINO THE ANSWER TO MY QUESTION OR NOT?

• •

Knock! Knock!
Who's there?
Chuckle.
Chuckle who?
Chuckle make you laugh, won't
you Chuck.

* *

Knock! Knock!
Who's there?
Mister E.
Mister E. who?
Mister E. meat is what they're serving for lunch today.

• • • • • • • • • • •

Knock! Knock!
Who's there?
Teller.
Teller who?
Teller fortune
for a dollar.

Knock! Knock!
Who's there?
Sieve.
Sieve who?
Sieve me a seat in the lunchroom.

Knock! Knock!
Who's there?
Hiatus.
Hiatus who?
Hiatus lunch and now the school bully
is after me.

Knock! Knock!
Who's there?
Sy.
Sy who?
Sy-los are good places to store grain.

KNOCK! KNOCK!
WHO'S THERE?
MERCEDES BENZ.
MERCEDES BENZ WHO?
MERCEDES BENZ STEEL IN
HER BARE HANDS.
SHE'S A SUPER GIRL.

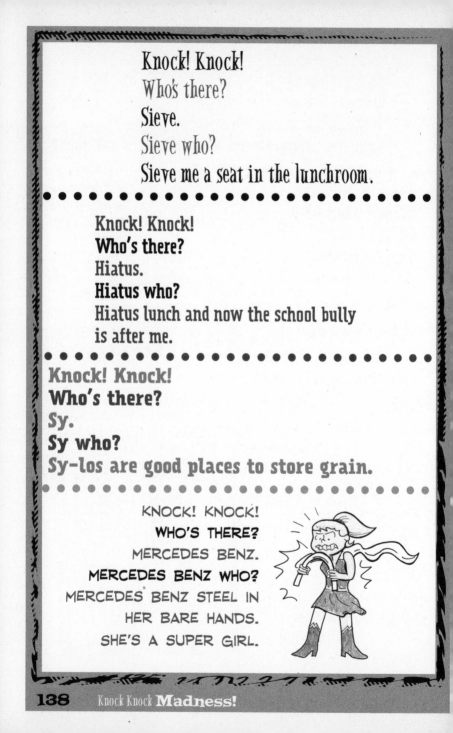

Knock! Knock!
Who's there?
A maid.
A maid who?
A maid you look!

• • • • • • • • • • • • • • • • • • • •

Knock! Knock!
Who's there?
Ida.
Ida who?
Ida made a terrific superhero.

• • • • • • • • • • • • • • • • • • • •

KNOCK! KNOCK!
WHO'S THERE?
ALPHABET.
ALPHABET WHO?
ALPHABET ME YOU'D SAY THAT.

• • • • • • • • • • • • • • • • • • • •

Knock! Knock!
Who's there?
Grin.
Grin who?
Grin you're smiling, the whole world smiles with you.

Knock! Knock!
Who's there?
Otto.
Otto who?
Otto mobile.

HEY! COME BACK HERE WITH MY OTTO!

KNOCK! KNOCK!
WHO'S THERE?
THATCHER.
THATCHER WHO?
THATCHER WAS A FUNNY STORY.

Knock! Knock!
Who's there?
Chair.
Chair who?
Chair up and don't be so gloomy.

Knock! Knock!
Who's there?
Beau Hen.
Beau Hen who?
Beau Hen Arrow.

KNOCK! KNOCK!
WHO'S THERE?
CANDIDATE.
CANDIDATE WHO?
CANDIDATE BE CHANGED TO SATURDAY NIGHT?

Knock! Knock!
Who's there?
Avenue.
Avenue who?
Avenue tried to get in here once before?

Knock! Knock!
Who's there?
Sayer.
Sayer who?
Sayer sorry.

Knock! Knock!
Who's there?
Sour.
Sour who?
Sour your parents doing these days?

Knock! Knock!
Who's there?
Seesaw.
Seesaw who?
Seesaw you sneak out last night.

* * * * * * * * *

Knock! Knock!
Who's there?
Vowel.
Vowel who?
**Vowel play is
suspected in this case.**

YOU HAVE THE RIGHT TO REMAIN SILENT!

* * * * * * * * * * * * *

Knock! Knock!
Who's there?
I lecture.
I lecture who?
I lecture dog out when I came in.

Knock! Knock!
Who's there?
Eclipse.
Eclipse who?
Eclipse my hair when it grows too long.

Knock! Knock!
Who's there?
Recycle.
Recycle who?
Recycle to work instead of driving cars.

* * * * * * * * * * * * * * * * * * *

KNOCK! KNOCK!
WHO'S THERE?
HEAVEN.
HEAVEN WHO?
HEAVEN YOU PLAYED ENOUGH VIDEO GAMES FOR ONE DAY?

Knock! Knock!
Who's there?
Butternut.
Butternut who?
Butternut change the channel. Mom's watching that show.

KNOCK! KNOCK!
WHO'S THERE?
DEBATE.
DEBATE WHO?
DEBATE FELL OFF MY HOOK. HAND ME A NEW WORM.

Knock! Knock!
Who's there?
Eddie.
Eddie who?
Eddie or not here I come.

• • • • • • • • • • • • • • • • • • • •

Knock! Knock!
Who's there?
Champ.
Champ who?
Champ who your hair at least once a week.

• • • • • • • • • • • • • • • • • • • •

Knock! Knock!
Who's there?
Cleaver.
Cleaver who?
Cleaver alone until she calms down.

• • • • • • • • • • • • • • • • • • • •

Knock! Knock!
Who's there?
I'm Igor.
I'm Igor who?
I'm Igor to begin our camping trip.

KNOCK! KNOCK!
WHO'S THERE?
PENCIL.
PENCIL WHO?
PENCIL FALL DOWN IF YOU
DON'T USE A BELT.

• •

Knock! Knock!
Who's there?
Irving.
Irving who?
Irving a great time, wish you were here.

• •

Knock! Knock!
Who's there?
Pete's.
Pete's who?
Pete's a pie delivery.
Open up.

JUST A MINUTE... I'LL BE RIGHT THERE...

• • • • • • • • • • • • • • • •

KNOCK! KNOCK!
WHO'S THERE?
JUST OODLE.
JUST OODLE WHO?
JUST OODLE YOU THINK
YOU'RE TALKING TO?

Knock! Knock!
Who's there?
Kerry.
Kerry who?
Kerry the groceries into the house.

KNOCK! KNOCK!
WHO'S THERE?
I PESO
I PESO WHO?
I PESO MUCH MONEY FOR RENT I
CAN'T AFFORD TO BUY GROCERIES.

Knock! Knock!
Who's there?
Hugo Whit.
Hugo Whit who?
Hugo whit mom. I'll go whit dad.

Knock! Knock!
Who's there?
Sid.
Sid who?
Sid over there in that easy chair.

KNOCK! KNOCK!
WHO'S THERE?
DIAL.
DIAL WHO?
DIAL NEVER BE ANOTHER YOU.

Knock! Knock!
Who's there?
Duet.
Duet who?
Duet yourself and quit bothering me.

Knock! Knock!
Who's there?
My April.
My April who?
My April show
you the way,
said Tarzan.

FOLLOW
ME!

Knock! Knock!
Who's there?
Russell.
Russell who?
Russell me up a snack, pardner.

Knock! Knock!
Who's there?
Artichokes.
Artichokes who?
Artichokes on food if
he eats too fast.

* *

Knock! Knock!
Who's there?
Rapper.
Rapper who?
Rapper up a sandwich to go.

* *

Knock! Knock!
Who's there?
Distress.
Distress who?
Distress matches my shoes and purse.

• •

KNOCK! KNOCK!
WHO'S THERE?
ARREST.
ARREST WHO?
ARREST ROOM SHOULD BE AT EVERY
TRUCK STOP.

Knock! Knock!
Who's there?
Hans.
Hans who?
Hans up and reach for the sky!

• •

Knock! Knock!
Who's there?
Luke.
Luke who?
Luke out below!

KNOCK! KNOCK!
WHO'S THERE?
SHALE.
SHALE WHO?
SHALE WE DANCE?

Knock! Knock!
Who's there?
Hans.
Hans who?
Hans off my dessert.

Knock! Knock!
Who's there?
Jacqueline.
Jacqueline who?
Jacqueline Hyde.

•••••••••••••••••••••••••

KNOCK! KNOCK!
WHO'S THERE?
RILEY.
RILEY WHO?
RILEY MAKES UP HIS MIND,
LET'S HUM A TUNE.

•••••••••••••••••••••••••

Knock! Knock!
Who's there?
Rot.
Rot who?
Rot do you want to do today?

•••••••••••••••••••••••••

Knock! Knock!
Who's there?
Bing.
Bing who?
Bing honest is a good way to live.

KNOCK! KNOCK!
WHO'S THERE?
BOW.
BOW WHO?
BOW YOUR
RUNNY NOSE.

• • • • • • • • • •

Knock! Knock!
Who's there?
Maryanne.
Maryanne who?
Maryanne I have a happy life together.

• • • • • • • • • • • • • • • • • • •

Knock! Knock!
Who's there?
Sinus.
Sinus who?
Sinus check for me.

• • • • • • • • • • • • • • • • • • •

Knock! Knock!
Who's there?
Sue.
Sue who?
Don't ask me. I'm not your lawyer.

Knock! Knock!
Who's there?
I'm Otter.
I'm Otter who?
I'm Otter answers.

****

Knock! Knock!
Who's there?
Dustbin.
Dustbin who?
Dustbin the worst day of my life.

Knock! Knock!
Who's there?
Lois Carmen.
Lois Carmen who?
Lois Carmen denominator.

KNOCK! KNOCK!
WHO'S THERE?
RIDDLE.
RIDDLE WHO?
RIDDLE YOUR MOTHER GETS HOME.

Knock! Knock!
Who's there?
Warrior.
Warrior who?
Warrior been all my life?

Knock! Knock!
Who's there?
Zenda.
Zenda who?
Zenda card to me on
my birthday.

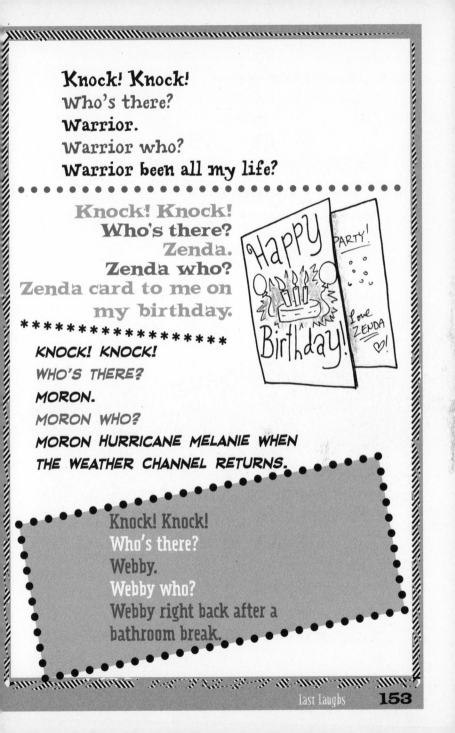

KNOCK! KNOCK!
WHO'S THERE?
MORON.
MORON WHO?
MORON HURRICANE MELANIE WHEN
THE WEATHER CHANNEL RETURNS.

Knock! Knock!
Who's there?
Webby.
Webby who?
Webby right back after a
bathroom break.

Knock! Knock!
Who's there?
Ibis.
Ibis who?
Ibis just leaving.

LATER, DUDE...

KNOCK! KNOCK!
WHO'S THERE?
LUCY.
LUCY WHO?
LUCY SEE WHAT CRAZY NEIGHBORS I HAVE?

Knock! Knock!
Who's there?
Ward.
Ward who?
Ward you consider opening a window?

Knock! Knock!
Who's there?
Rachel.
Rachel who?
Rachel equality is a good thing.

KNOCK! KNOCK!
WHO'S THERE?
WILLIS.
WILLIS WHO?
WILLIS FRIENDS STICK UP FOR HIM?

Knock! Knock!
Who's there?
Hugh Noah Howe.
Hugh Noah Howe who?
Hugh Noah Howe mad I can get.

Knock! Knock!
Who's there?
Hunger.
Hunger who?
Hunger wet clothes on the line to dry.

Knock! Knock!
Who's there?
I flounder.
I flounder who?
I flounder hiding in the bushes.

KNOCK! KNOCK!
WHO'S THERE?
RAISIN.
RAISIN WHO?
RAISIN CHILDREN IS A DIFFICULT JOB.

Knock! Knock!
Who's there?
Counsel.
Counsel who?
Counsel my reservation. I'm not going.

Knock! Knock!
Who's there?
Walker.
Walker who?
Walker home after
the party.

KNOCK! KNOCK!
WHO'S THERE?
SHAW.
SHAW WHO?
SHAW YOU AT SCHOOL YESTERDAY.

Knock! Knock!
Who's there?
Locate.
Locate who?
Locate or would you rather I
say Hello Kathleen?

• • • • • • • • • • • • • • • • • • • •

Knock! Knock!
Who's there?
Harriet.
Harriet who?
Harriet too much. He's such a glutton.

• • • • • • • • • • • • • • • • • • • •

Knock! Knock!
Who's there?
Caesar.
Caesar who?
Caesar! She's wanted
by the F.B.I.

WANTED
BY THE F.B.I.

REWARD!

• • • • • • • • • • • • • •

Knock! Knock!
Who's there?
Your boat.
Your boat who?
Your boat to blame for this big mess.

Knock! Knock!
Who's there?
Luwanna.
Luwanna who?
Luwanna go to a movie with me?

* * * * * * * * * * * * * * * * * *

KNOCK! KNOCK!
WHO'S THERE?
YODA.
YODA WHO?
YODA LADY HOO!!

* * * * * * * *

Knock! Knock!
Who's there?
Francie.
Francie who?
Francie meeting you here.

* *

Knock! Knock!
Who's there?
Candice.
Candice who?
Candice be just a silly mistake?

KNOCK! KNOCK!
WHO'S THERE?
REEF.
REEF WHO?
REEF JUST MOVED IN NEXT DOOR.

* * * * * * * * * * * * * * * * * *

Knock! Knock!
Who's there?
Cartoon.
Cartoon who?
Cartoon ups make your engine run well.

Knock! Knock!
Who's there?
Albert.
Albert who?
Albert you don't remember me.

Knock! Knock!
Who's there?
Return.
Return who?
Return right at the next traffic light.

About Applesauce Press

WHAT KID DOESN'T LOVE APPLESAUCE?

APPLESAUCE PRESS WAS CREATED TO PRESS OUT THE BEST CHILDREN'S BOOKS FOUND ANYWHERE. LIKE OUR PARENT COMPANY, CIDER MILL PRESS BOOK PUBLISHERS, WE STRIVE TO BRING FINE READING, INFORMATION, AND ENTERTAINMENT TO KIDS OF ALL AGES. BETWEEN THE COVERS OF OUR CREATIVELY CRAFTED BOOKS, YOU'LL FIND BEAUTIFUL DESIGNS, CREATIVE FORMATS, AND MOST OF ALL, KID-FRIENDLY INFORMATION ON A VARIETY OF TOPICS. OUR CIDER MILL BEARS FRUIT TWICE A YEAR, PUBLISHING A NEW CROP OF TITLES EACH SPRING AND FALL.

"WHERE GOOD BOOKS ARE READY FOR PRESS"

VISIT US ON THE WEB AT
WWW.CIDERMILLPRESS.COM
OR WRITE TO US AT
12 PORT FARM ROAD
KENNEBUNKPORT, MAINE 04046